Radiation

&

Human Health

Navigating the Digital Age of Gadgets

and Wireless Networks for a Safer

Tomorrow

SUBURU NOMMO ISHMAEL

Contents

Description..3

Introduction..7

Chapter 1: The Digital Revolution...10

Chapter 2: Understanding Radiation......................................13

Chapter 3: Health Issues and Debates....................................17

Chapter 4: Minimizing Exposure...20

Chapter 5: Convenience and Caution......................................24

Chapter 6: Technological Innovations 28

Chapter 7: Convenience and Caution......................................32

Choosing a Mindful Digital Future as a Finality 36

Conclusion 38

LIST OF Practical Steps 40

Description

We live in a technological age when there is no shortage of devices that have changed the way we communicate, work, and interact with the outside world. Our lives are more intertwined with technology than ever, from cell phones that keep us continuously linked to Wi-Fi networks that power our houses. But although we enjoy the modern comforts, concerns regarding the dangers of radiation from these devices to our health have surfaced.

The problem of radiation and its effects on human health has never been more pertinent in a society where digital devices are completely incorporated into our everyday lives. A thorough investigation of the complex connection between technology and our well-being may be found in "Radiation & Human Health: Navigating the Digital Age of Gadgets for a Safer Tomorrow."

We go through the heart of the digital age in this insightful book, where gadgets are our devoted friends, boosting our productivity, tying us to our loved ones, and opening a portal to the outside world. Thoughts concerning the electromagnetic radiation that these devices generate and its possible consequences on our health are there beneath this dazzling surface.

We dig into the realm of gadget radiation, demystifying its various forms and comprehending its ramifications, from mobile phones to Wi-Fi routers, from wearable technology to smart homes. We sift through the maze of scholarly discussions, conflicts, and arguments to give you a fair overview of the subject.

Your full resource for comprehending and tackling these issues is "Radiation & Human Health: Navigating the Digital Age of Gadgets for a Safer Tomorrow." We go through the digital age's core, where technology and well-being collide, in this illuminating book.

Dispelling Myths About Gadget Radiation

We begin by exploring the complex realm of device radiation. We break down the many forms of radiation to help you understand their consequences for your health, from the radiofrequency waves released by cell phones to the electromagnetic fields of our smart homes.

Combining Convenience with Care:

However, this book is about empowering rather than merely voicing concerns. We provide you with workable solutions to reduce your radiation exposure while maximizing the benefits of the digital age. Learn how to establish safer digital environments in your house, form wholesome usage patterns, and safeguard the welfare of your family.

Technology Advancements for a Safer Future:

Innovations to lower radiation emissions also progress along with technology. Learn about the newest advancements in gadget security and look at wearable technology that puts your health first. We keep you up to date on cutting-edge innovations that are transforming how we use technology and fostering a more secure digital future.

A blueprint for mindful online living is as follows:

We arrive at a vision of mindful digital life at the end of our adventure. This book gives insightful information, practical suggestions, and a road map to a safer future, whether you're a tech enthusiast, a worried parent, or just someone intrigued about the world of electronics and radiation.

Join us on an educational tour of the technology, radiation, and health worlds. Together, we'll navigate the digital era with discernment, caution, and a dedication to creating a future in which well-being and technology coexist together. Your manual for utilizing the benefits of technology while preserving your health and the welfare of people you care about is "Radiation & Human Health: Navigating the Digital Age of Gadgets for a Safer Tomorrow."

Start here to find a safer digital future.

Introduction

Our life and technology are linked in the twenty-first century. Our daily lives are characterized by an ever-expanding digital landscape, from the pervasiveness of smartphones and the convenience of laptops to the spread of intelligent appliances and the rise of the Internet of Things (IoT). Although these technological developments have improved our lives in terms of ease and connectedness, they have also given rise to a growing worry about the radiation generated by these devices and their possible effects on human health.

We now live in a world where technology is our daily companion thanks to the digital revolution. For communication, information, entertainment, and even health monitoring, we rely on them. But underneath the flawless interfaces and slick screens are intricate processes that produce different kinds of radiation. Even though these emissions are frequently invisible to the human eye, concerns have been raised regarding how they can affect our health.

With the help of this book, we will go on an important journey through the digital world and examine the complex link between gadget radiation and human health.

We explore the science of radiation, examine the studies that sparked controversy, and identify the doable steps people can take to reduce dangers while using the advantages of our constantly linked world.

The chapters that follow will shed light on the radiation spectrum, defining ionizing and non-ionizing radiation, and provide a thorough explanation of the numerous types released by our devices. We will navigate the ongoing debates and research that have stoked worries to bring clarity to a sea of contradictory data.

Furthermore, this book is a guide to making educated decisions rather than a call to fear or worry. It includes a look at emerging technologies intended to reduce dangers, a discussion of vulnerable populations, and an investigation into safe usage methods. Striking a balance between the ease that technology affords and the prudence needed to protect our health is a challenge.

It's crucial to keep in mind that technology is not the enemy and that gadget radiation is not an insurmountable menace as we set out on this adventure. It serves as a reminder of the importance of education and making wise decisions. It is an opportunity to investigate how we might securely navigate the digital era, utilizing technology's transformational potential while safeguarding the priceless gift of our health for present and future generations.

Chapter 1: The Digital Revolution

Few events in the vast scope of human history have left an imprint as permanent as the digital revolution. The landscape of human existence has changed dramatically with the invention of the World Wide Web, cell phones, and the rise of artificial intelligence. As we navigate the landscape of the twenty-first century, we discover that we are engulfed in a digital world that is changing the way we think, live, work, and communicate.

Historical Considerations

The creation of the first computers in the middle of the 20th century catalyzed this digital revolution. These enormous systems served as the forerunners to today's sleek and portable electronics with their sophisticated networks of vacuum tubes and reels of magnetic tape. By proposing the idea of processing information using binary code—a language of ones and zeros that serves as the basis of contemporary computing—they opened the way for the digital age.

The pace of technological development expanded tremendously in the decades that followed. Computers became more approachable and user-friendly with the introduction of microprocessors, the downsizing of components, and the development of graphical user interfaces. The advent of the internet brought about unprecedented levels of global connectivity.

The Pervasiveness of Devices

The widespread use of electronic devices is one of the hallmarks of the digital revolution. From smartphones and tablets to smartwatches and fitness trackers, these gadgets have evolved into necessary daily tools. They act as access points for data, channels for communication, and entry points for enjoyment. With their convenience, connectedness, and unheard-of powers, devices have become our constant companions, whether we're navigating city streets, holding business meetings, or keeping track of our health.

The Radiation Mysteries

But underlying these devices' svelte exteriors and brilliant displays comes a complicated reality—a reality of radiation. Gadgets produce radiation in a variety of ways as they carry out their many duties, which has raised questions and sparked discussions about potential health dangers.

Our journey starts right here, at the nexus of technology and health. We shall explore the various types of radiation emitted by gadgets and analyze the science that supports our understanding of their impacts on human health in this book to solve the mystery of gadget radiation. We will examine the research, the viewpoints of the experts, and the industry's answers as we delve into the controversy that surrounds this subject.

Beyond the discussion, however, this book serves as a practical manual and invitation to travel safely in the digital age. It will include information on how people can make wise decisions, establish safe usage habits, and protect their health and the health of those they care about. Striking a balance between the necessity to reduce potential hazards and the clear advantages of technology is the goal.

We recognize that the digital revolution is more than just a section of human history; it is the key event in our era as we set out on this voyage into the digital world. It has the potential to reinvent the human experience, reshape society, and democratize knowledge. And while we accept this transition, we have to do so with discernment, caution, and a firm dedication to our health and well-being.

Chapter 2: Understanding Radiation

In our exploration of the potential impact of gadget radiation on human health, it is essential to lay a solid foundation by understanding the nature of radiation itself. This chapter is dedicated to shedding light on the different types of radiation, both ionizing and non-ionizing and how they relate to the digital devices we use daily.

The Electromagnetic Spectrum

The radiation emitted by gadgets falls within the realm of electromagnetic radiation, which encompasses a broad spectrum of energy waves. At one end of this spectrum, we find low-energy radio waves and microwaves. In the middle, we encounter visible light, the spectrum of colors that our eyes can perceive. And at the high-energy end, we have X-rays and gamma rays.

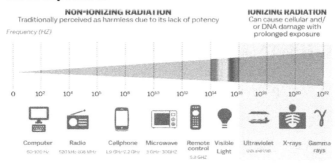

The radiation on the electromagnetic spectrum we're exposed to

Radiation that is ionizing versus non-ionizing

The contrast between ionizing and non-ionizing radiation is essential to comprehending radiation.

Radiation that is ionizing High energy levels in this type of radiation are sufficient to ionize atoms and molecules by removing the electrons from them. Ionizing radiation is exemplified by X-rays and gamma rays. Ionizing radiations have a high energy and can seriously harm biological tissues. When exposed in excess, they are also linked to a higher risk of developing cancer.

Non-ionizing radiation, on the other hand, is devoid of the energy necessary to ionize atoms or molecules. Instead, it causes the molecules in the matter to vibrate or rotate, which produces heat. Radiofrequency (RF) radiation, microwaves, and visible light are all examples of non-ionizing radiation. These radiation types are typically regarded as less dangerous than ionizing radiation.

Devices and Non-ionizing Radiation Types

We are particularly concerned with non-ionizing radiation, specifically radiofrequency (RF) radiation, and microwaves, as we concentrate on the effects of gadget radiation.

1. Radiofrequency (RF) Radiation: A variety of wireless gadgets, such as cell phones, Wi-Fi routers, and Bluetooth devices, emit RF radiation. Wireless communication is made possible by these emissions, but considering how close to our bodies they are while in use, there are worries about potential health repercussions.

2. Microwaves: As the name implies, microwaves are used to cook food in microwave ovens. They are also released by satellites, radar systems, and cell towers. Microwaves can transfer vast amounts of data due to their wavelengths, but their implications on human health are still being researched and debated.

RF Radiation's Absorption

How our bodies absorb radiation from gadgets is a crucial factor to comprehend.

1. The RF radiation that wireless gadgets, particularly cell phones, release while we use them is absorbed by the tissues closest to the device. This indicates that when a cell phone is held close to the ear, the cranium and brain are the main absorption sites.

2.

2. Microwaves: As the name implies, microwaves are used to cook food in microwave ovens. They are also released by satellites, radar systems, and cell towers. Microwaves can transfer vast amounts of data due to their wavelengths, but their implications on human health are still being researched and debated.

RF Radiation's Absorption

How our bodies absorb radiation from gadgets is a crucial factor to comprehend. The RF radiation that wireless gadgets, particularly cell phones, release while we use them is absorbed by the tissues closest to the device. This indicates that when a cell phone is held close to the ear, the cranium and brain are the main absorption sites.

Chapter 3: Health Issues and Debates

Explore the health issues and controversies that have emerged in this complicated environment as we delve deeper into the complexities of gadget radiation and its possible impact on human health. The controversies, research, and current conversations around the negative health impacts of radiation generated by electronic gadgets are better understood through the perspective of this chapter.

The Debate Concerning RF Radiation

Radiofrequency (RF) radiation, the kind of non-ionizing radiation released by cell phones, Wi-Fi routers, and other wireless gadgets, is one of the major topics of discussion in the area of gadget radiation. While some research relates RF radiation exposure to specific health problems, other studies find little to no evidence of harm. Study methodology, different takes on the data, and the power of special interests all contribute to the complexity of this debate.

Cell phones and brain tumor research

The link between chronic cell phone use and the incidence of brain cancers is a major point of debate. Studies have shown that there is a higher risk, especially for people who use their phones for long periods. Although many experts contend that further research is necessary to establish a solid connection, these results are not generally regarded as conclusive.

Hypersensitivity to electromagnetic fields (EHS)

Electromagnetic hypersensitivity (EHS), a condition in which people claim to experience a variety of symptoms—such as headaches, exhaustion, and skin rashes—in reaction to exposure to electromagnetic fields, is another hotly debated subject. The scientific community is still split on whether EHS is psychological in origin or induced by electromagnetic radiation, although some patients with these symptoms are genuinely incapacitated.

Influence of Industry: Its Function

The involvement of industry in this debate adds still another level of complexity. There have been questions regarding the objectivity of research done and supported by the electronics and telecommunications industries due to the significant financial stakes involved. As a result, several research' dependability has come under scrutiny.

Using caution is recommended

The precautionary principle stands out as a key idea amid these discussions and squabbles. In the face of scientific ambiguity, this principle encourages taking preventive measures, especially when dealing with potential hazards to the public's health. Even in the absence of solid proof of danger, it promotes prudent behaviors and policies that err on the side of caution.

The Next Steps

It is difficult to make sense of the health issues and controversy concerning gadget radiation. It necessitates critical thinking, an understanding of the limitations of scientific study, and a desire to keep up with discoveries. The chapters that follow will go into detail about how to reduce potential threats from gadget radiation while still taking advantage of technology. We keep in mind as we investigate that, despite the ongoing controversy, the search for information and the use of the precautionary principle continue to serve as our compass points.

Chapter 4: Minimizing Exposure

One significant issue emerges in the complex web of discussions and worries regarding gadget radiation and its possible effects on human health: How can people take actionable actions to reduce their exposure while enjoying the benefits of the digital age? Actionable advice on reducing exposure to gadget radiation is the focus of this chapter.

Safe Use Techniques

1. Mobile Phone Safety: Considering how commonplace cell phone use is, it's crucial to follow safe usage habits. Use loudspeaker mode or a corded headset to keep the phone away from your head, send texts instead of calls when you can, and cut back on the number of calls you make overall.

2. Wi-Fi safety: Wi-Fi routers produce RF radiation, and while research on their health effects is ongoing, it is recommended to keep routers out of bedrooms, switch off Wi-Fi when not in use, and connect stationary equipment to Ethernet instead of wireless networks.

3. Limit Screen Time: Reducing screen time on devices like tablets and laptops can offer several advantages, including lowering exposure to displays' low levels of non-ionizing radiation. Encourage screen-free activities and breaks, especially for young children.

4. Keep Gadgets at a Distance: Keep wireless gadgets at a distance while not in use. Avoid carrying a mobile phone in a pocket that is near to the body, and use tables instead of your lap while using a laptop.

Hypersensitivity to electromagnetic fields (EHS)

There are further actions people can take if they think they are electromagnetic field sensitive and exhibit symptoms of EHS:

1. Reduce Exposure: Identify EMF sources and reduce exposure to them. This can entail using fewer wireless gadgets, sticking with conventional connections, and designating specific areas of the house as EMF-free zones.

2. Speak with a medical expert: For help managing symptoms and making lifestyle changes, see a medical expert with expertise in environmental medicine or EMF sensitivity.

Protecting Vulnerable Populations

Certain populations are more vulnerable to the potential effects of gadget radiation, including children and pregnant individuals. For these groups:

1. Children: Encourage responsible gadget usage for children. Limit screen time, educate them about safe practices, and consider using parental control features on devices.

2. Pregnant Individuals: Minimize gadget use during pregnancy, especially devices that emit RF radiation like cell phones, near the belly. Consider using a speakerphone or a wired headset during calls.

Exercising caution is recommended

The precautionary principle, which was covered in Chapter 3, is crucial in reducing exposure. Following this rule enables people to take preventive action, such as cutting back on device use when safer alternatives are available and implementing safer habits, even in the absence of solid proof of damage.

Conclusion of Exposure Minimization

While there are still ongoing discussions concerning gadget radiation and its possible health implications, people may actively lower their exposure by adopting safe usage habits, making settings free of EMFs, and taking the needs of sensitive groups into account. By doing this, they manage to maintain a balance between embracing technology and protecting their own and their loved ones' health—a balance that enables them to move through the digital era with sagacity and caution.

Chapter 5: Convenience and Caution

Finding a careful balance between the ease and benefits of technology and the cautious approach needed to protect one's health is a constant challenge while navigating the digital age and the complicated world of gadget radiation. This chapter investigates methods and factors to keep this balance in our digital life.

Encouragement of Technology Literacy

1. Digital Education: It's crucial to encourage technological literacy. People may make better decisions if they are taught how to use technology responsibly and safely, especially youngsters. This entails being aware of possible threats, following safe digital practices, and comprehending how technologies operate.

2. Encourage critical thinking on how technology affects daily living. Encouragement of inquiries on the necessity of technology usage in diverse contexts might result in thoughtful device use.

Mindfulness and Digital Detox

1. Digital detox: Periodic breaks from screens and gadgets, during which people purposefully unplug, can be very helpful. These detoxes offer chances to rest,

concentrate on face-to-face interactions, and lower overall exposure to gadget radiation.

2. Mindfulness Techniques: Including mindfulness techniques in everyday activities might assist people in being more conscious of their device usage. Mindfulness encourages being present at the moment and can aid in recognizing when digital distractions are taking away from meaningful experiences.

Creating Limits

Establish screen-free zones in your house by designating places like the dining room table and the bedroom as such. These areas can operate as safe havens from gadget radiation, encouraging sounder sleep and more beneficial social connections.

2. Designate particular periods during the day when electronics are put away, such as before bed or during meals. These intermissions offer the chance for relaxation and family time without technology.

Digital Tools for Well-Being

Apps and features built into devices that track usage may be used to monitor screen time and app usage. Making deliberate decisions about using gadgets is made easier with the help of these technologies, which offer insights into digital behaviors.

2. Parental Controls: To maintain a better balance between technology usage and other activities, parental control tools can assist families in controlling their children's screen time and content access.

Promoting Technological Advancements

1. Safer Technologies: Keep up with new developments that try to cut down on radiation emissions from electronics. These developments aim to deliver technology's advantages with the fewest possible health dangers.

2. Wearable Technology: Discover the world of wearable technology, including fitness trackers and smartwatches, that promotes health and well-being. Comparing these gadgets to cell phones, their radiation emissions are frequently lower.

Policy and Advocacy

1. Activism Participate in lobbying campaigns that support smart device use and production. Supporting groups and projects aimed at ensuring the safety of gadget radiation can improve market norms.

2. Administration Policies: Keep up with government laws and rules about radiation guidelines for electronics. Promote strict rules that put consumer safety first.

Conclusion

A talent that both people and families may develop is the capacity to strike a balance between the convenience of technology and the prudent use of gadgets. People may manage the digital age with more awareness and control by promoting technological literacy, engaging in mindfulness practices, setting boundaries, making use of digital well-being tools, and learning about safer technologies.

This chapter emphasizes the significance of deliberate and considerate technology usage, encouraging a positive interaction with technology that improves well-being rather than jeopardizes it. With the help of these techniques, people may make use of the digital world's benefits while maintaining a balanced lifestyle that is consistent with their beliefs and objectives.

Chapter 6: Technological Innovations

Technological advancements hold the key to resolving worries about gadget radiation and its possible effects on human health in a digital environment that is continually expanding. This chapter examines new developments and technology intended to cut radiation emissions and encourage safe gadget use.

Safer Technology for Devices

Low-Radiation Equipment: More companies are creating technology with fewer radiation emissions. These gadgets are made to meet or even surpass safety requirements, giving customers choices that put their health first.

2. Radiation Shielding: Some modern gadgets have radiation shielding integrated into them. These shields are designed to lessen the radiation exposure to the user while the gadget is in use.

3. Reduced Power Modes: When gadgets are in standby or low-power modes, radiation emissions are reduced via energy-efficient features. This reduces unwanted radiation exposure while simultaneously conserving energy.

Health Monitoring and Wearable Technology

1. Smartwatches: Due to their capacity to monitor health metrics without necessitating continual smartphone usage, smartwatches and wearable fitness trackers have become more popular. Comparing these gadgets to cell phones, their radiation emissions are frequently lower.

2. Remote Health Monitoring: With the use of telehealth and remote health monitoring tools, people may keep tabs on their health without often visiting medical facilities. By reducing the need for continuous smartphone use, these solutions may limit radiation exposure.

Home Connectivity and IoT Security

1. Safety of IoT devices: As the Internet of Things (IoT) develops, manufacturers are urged to create IoT products with a focus on security. The development of these gadgets is increasingly focused on ensuring that they release as little radiation as possible.

2. IoT Data Security: As the number of linked households increases, it is crucial to protect personal information and maintain privacy. Strong data security procedures may be implemented to reduce any hazards connected to IoT devices.

Modern Innovations

1. 5G and Beyond: As 5G technology is introduced, it makes promises of communication that is quicker and more effective. However, worries about the rising number of cell towers and their possible negative impacts on health have been voiced. It is crucial to do ongoing studies and conduct sound infrastructure planning.

2. Biocompatible Materials: Some studies investigate the application of biocompatible materials in gadget design. These materials might be used in the creation of new devices in the future since they are designed to lessen the body's absorption of radiation.

Innovation and Caution in Balance

Although these developments provide hope for a safer digital future, it is crucial to view them from a fair angle. Continuous investigation and watchfulness are needed to evaluate the long-term safety of emerging technology. Consumers must make educated decisions by staying informed about the possible advantages and hazards of new advances.

The safety of developing technology is also significantly influenced by governmental rules and industry norms. Supporting strict laws and ethical production procedures helps ensure that consumer health is given priority in technology breakthroughs.

The technological innovations have concluded.

Innovation will determine the safety of gadget radiation in the future. People and society may continue to benefit from the conveniences of the digital era while reducing possible health hazards by adopting developing technologies that lower radiation emissions, monitoring health through wearable devices, and pushing for ethical behaviors.

This chapter emphasizes the innovation's role in fostering a safer and more interconnected world as well as the changing character of the digital landscape. Consumers must remain educated and involved as technology develops to actively influence its future trajectory in ways that favor security and well-being.

Chapter 7: Convenience and Caution

It's critical to establish a balance between the benefits and convenience of technology and the care needed to protect our health in the digital era, where devices have become indispensable. The practical methods and factors to keep this balance are examined in this chapter.

Encouragement of Technology Literacy

1. Digital Education: It's crucial to encourage technological literacy. Teach people, especially kids, how to use technology responsibly and safely. This entails developing sound digital habits, being aware of possible threats, and comprehending how technologies operate.

2. Encourage critical thinking on how technology affects daily living: Encouragement of inquiries on the necessity of technology usage in diverse contexts might result in thoughtful device use.

Mindfulness and Digital Detox

1. Digital detox: Periodic breaks from screens and gadgets, during which people purposefully unplug, may be quite helpful. These detoxes offer chances to rest, concentrate on face-to-face interactions, and lower overall exposure to gadget radiation.

2. Mindfulness Techniques: Including mindfulness techniques in everyday activities might assist people in being more conscious of their device usage. Being mindful may help you recognize when digital distractions are taking away from valuable experiences by encouraging you to be in the now.

Creating Limits

Establish screen-free zones in your house by designating places like the dining room table and the bedroom as such. These areas can operate as safe havens from gadget radiation, encouraging sounder sleep and more beneficial social connections.

2. Designate particular periods during the day when electronics are put away, such as before bed or during meals. These intermissions offer the chance for relaxation and family time without technology.

Digital Tools for Well-Being

1. Apps and features built into devices that track usage may be used to monitor screen time and app usage. Making deliberate decisions about using gadgets is made easier with the help of these technologies, which offer insights into digital behaviors.

2. Parental Controls: To maintain a better balance between technology usage and other activities, parental control tools can assist families in controlling their children's screen time and content access.

Promoting technological advancements

1. Safer Technologies: Keep up with new developments that try to cut down on radiation emissions from electronics. These developments aim to deliver technology's advantages with the fewest possible health dangers.

2. Wearable Technology: Discover the world of wearable technology, including fitness trackers and smartwatches, that promotes health and well-being. Comparing these gadgets to cell phones, their radiation emissions are frequently lower.

Policy and Advocacy

1. Advocacy: Participate in advocacy campaigns that support responsible gadget use and production. Supporting groups and projects aimed at ensuring the safety of gadget radiation can improve market norms.

2. Administration Policies: Keep up with government laws and rules about radiation guidelines for electronics. Promote strict rules that put consumer safety first.

Conclusion

A talent that both individuals and families may develop is the capacity to strike a balance between the convenience of technology and the prudent use of gadgets. People may manage the digital age with more awareness and control by promoting technological literacy, engaging in mindfulness practices, setting boundaries, making use of digital well-being tools, and learning about safer technologies.

This chapter emphasizes the significance of deliberate and considerate technology usage, encouraging a positive interaction with technology that improves well-being rather than jeopardizes it. With the help of these techniques, people may make use of the digital world's benefits while maintaining a balanced lifestyle that is consistent with their beliefs and objectives.

Choosing a Mindful Digital Future as a Finality

The digital era is a chapter of extraordinary change in the broad fabric of human existence. Technology has influenced every aspect of our lives, from the creation of the computer to the pervasive cell phones that connect us across continents. It's important to take stock of our investigation into gadget radiation and its effects on our health as we approach the dawn of this new age.

Taking Stock of Progress

We have discovered the complex network of gadget radiation along the way—its varieties, its impacts, and the continuous discussions over its safety. We have looked at ways to reduce exposure and provide a secure online environment. While discussing concerns and safety measures, it's important to acknowledge the indisputable advancements technology has made in our lives.

We have observed how technological advancements have reshaped businesses, democratized information, and modernized communication. Technology has acted as a catalyst for progress, connecting patients with remote healthcare professionals through telemedicine and empowering students of all ages through educational resources.

Accepting Individuality

As we draw to a close, it's critical to understand that everyone's experience with technology is different. What functions well for one person or family might not be appropriate for another. As a result, no one method works for everyone to stay secure in the digital era. Instead, it's about accepting our individuality and making decisions that are consistent with our priorities and core beliefs.

It involves striking a balance between the benefits and convenience of technology and the care needed to protect our health and well-being. We can leverage the force of innovation while being aware of possible hazards thanks to this balance.

Future of the Mindful Digital

Let's embrace a conscious digital future as we go toward a more connected society. Let us:

1. We empower ourselves and the following generation to utilize technology responsibly by encouraging technological literacy and critical thinking.

2. Engage in mindfulness exercises: Mindfulness exercises help us to be mindful of the present moment and

to discern when technology is enhancing or detracting from life's meaningful experiences.

3. Establish Limits: By designating screen-free areas and times, we can keep a healthy balance between our online and offline relationships.

4. Make use of tools for digital well-being: Parental controls and tracking applications offer insightful management information and assistance.

5. Support Innovation Responsibly: Advocate for consumer protection rules and practices while embracing developing technologies that put safety and well-being first.

6. Stay Informed and Active: Continue to educate yourself on the most recent technological advancements and how they affect your life. Positive changes to the digital world may result from active participation in lobbying and policy campaigns.

Conclusion

Let's not forget that technology is a tool that we can use to sculpt our future. It is a driving force for development, a wellspring of creativity, and a link that unites people from different backgrounds and cultures. We can make sure that technology continues to improve our lives, build connections, and increase our collective well-being by adopting a conscious attitude to our digital interactions.

Let's proceed into this bright new digital world with caution, discernment, and a firm commitment to the principles that are most important to us. We are still on our trip, and the direction we take will determine how the digital era will be for future generations.

List of Practical Steps

Practical steps you can take to navigate the digital age of gadgets for a safer tomorrow in the context of radiation and human health:

Minimizing Exposure

1. Use speakerphone or wired headsets for phone calls to keep the device away from your head.

2. Text instead of making lengthy phone calls when possible.

3. Reduce call times and frequency, especially for long conversations.

4. Turn off Wi-Fi when not in use to limit exposure from routers.

5. Place Wi-Fi routers in central locations away from bedrooms.

6. Use Ethernet connections for stationary devices like computers.

7. Limit screen time, especially for children.

8. Encourage regular breaks from screens to reduce exposure.

9. Avoid carrying a cell phone in pockets close to your body.

10. Place laptops on tables instead of laps to reduce exposure.

11. Use airplane mode when not actively using your smartphone.

12. Keep wireless devices at a distance when not in use.

13. Turn off gadgets and Wi-Fi at night to promote restful sleep.

14. Consider using wired devices like landline phones when possible.

15. Create EMF-free zones in your home, especially in bedrooms.

Tech Literacy and Awareness

16. Educate yourself and your family about gadget radiation.

17. Stay informed about the latest research on radiation and health.

18. Understand the differences between various types of gadget radiation.

19. Recognize the potential risks associated with gadget radiation.

20. Encourage critical thinking about the necessity of technology use.

21. Teach children responsible gadget usage and healthy digital habits.

22. Promote digital literacy and safe online behavior.

Zones and Times Without Screens

23. Set aside areas of your home without screens (e.g., dining table, bedroom).

Set aside some hours each day to avoid using screens (e.g., meals, before bedtime).

25. Establish family time without technology to promote interpersonal relationships.

Mindfulness and Digital Detox

26. Practice digital detox by occasionally turning off your screen.

27. Practice mindfulness to increase your awareness of how you use your devices.

28. Create times during the day when no devices are used to recharge.

29. Establish a conscious connection with technology.

Use digital tools for well-being

30. Track your device usage using built-in applications that track your screen time.

Set time restrictions for individual apps to cut down on screen time.

To reduce distractions, turn on "Do Not Disturb" mode.

33. Investigate parental control options to limit kids' screen time.

34. Keep track of your daily screen time and try to cut it back gradually.

35. Make use of applications that assist you in keeping a balanced digital lifc.

Encourage safer technology

36. Find devices with reduced radiation emissions and select them.

37. Choose gadgets with built-in radiation protection systems.

38. To decrease radiation, choose devices with low power settings.

39. Take into account adopting wearable technology with fewer emissions, such as smartwatches.

Policy and Advocacy

40. Participate in advocacy campaigns for ethical gadget production.

41. Support groups dedicated to ensuring the safety of electronic radiation.

42. Maintain up-to-date knowledge of governmental radiation standards rules and laws.

43. Speak up in favor of strict rules that put consumer protection first.

Tech-Healthy Habits

44. Reduce screen time for gaming and other activities.

45. Encourage kids to play outside and engage in physical activity.

46. Limit smartphone use when the family is eating.

47. Give in-person encounters more importance than online ones.

48. Exercise caution when using electronics in public.

49. Make useful and instructional use of technology.

50. Take stock of your technology usage patterns and make deliberate decisions.

regular health examinations

51. Arrange routine medical exams to keep an eye on your general health.

52. Talk to your healthcare physician about any worries you have concerning device radiation exposure.

If you suffer symptoms of electromagnetic hypersensitivity, you might want to speak with a medical expert who specializes in environmental medicine or EMF sensitivity (EHS).

Taking Care of Vulnerable Populations

54. Create rules and restrictions for kids' responsible gadget usage.

55. Inform kids about the radiation exposure and excessive screen time concerns.

56. To regulate the material and usage of children, use parental control options.

57. Encourage women who are pregnant to use technology less, especially when it comes to items that are near the belly.

58. When making phone calls when pregnant, use a speakerphone or a corded headset.

Remain informed and involved

59. Stay current on radiation safety and technological advancements.

60. Continue to participate in online forums and groups devoted to device safety.

61. Encourage scientific investigation on the connection between gadget radiation and health.

62. To spread awareness, educate your friends and family about your expertise and views.

Digital-Free Retreats

63. To detach from screens and technology, schedule tech-free weekends or vacations.

64. Look for pastimes and pursuits free of modern gadgets.

65. Recharge by spending time in nature and engaging in outdoor activities.

Safe Children's Devices

66. Look into and choose gadgets with safety features and low radiation levels that are specially made for kids.

67. Choosing kid-friendly applications and content is step number 67.

Encourage kids to utilize technology creatively and educationally.

69. For extremely young children, limit their exposure to screens and technology.

Update Safety Measures Frequently

70. Keep abreast of safety advice and guidelines about gadget radiation.

71. As technology and devices advance, review and tweak your safety precautions.

72. Consider purchasing technology that has updated security features and lower radiation emissions.

Encourage digital well-being in classrooms

73. Speak up in favor of teaching students about responsible technology use through digital well-being education in the classroom.

Encourage schools to include screen-free periods in their schedules.

75. Encourage tech wellness and literacy programs at educational institutions.

Public Awareness

76. Host or take part in neighborhood workshops and lectures on tech safety.

77. Increase public awareness of the dangers of excessive technology use.

78. Collaborate with regional groups to advance the ethical use of technology.

Set a good example

79. Show your family and friends how to use technology responsibly and politely.

80. Give face-to-face encounters in social contexts precedence over digital ones.

81. Demonstrate that it is feasible to take advantage of technology's advantages while being aware of its potential negative effects on health.

Promote the use of safer technology

82. Encourage manufacturers to give safety and lowered radiation emissions priority while designing gadgets.

83. Participate in initiatives that urge device makers to reveal their radiation emissions.

84. Work with lawmakers to promote rules that place a high priority on consumer safety in the digital sector.

Encourage mindful online behavior

85. Tell people about your efforts to live a mindful online life.

Encourage your family and friends to have a well-rounded view of technology.

87. Honor the advantages of ethical technology use in your locality.

It is everyone's job to navigate the digital era of devices for a safer tomorrow. These doable actions provide you the freedom to embrace the digital era while defending your health and well-being in a radiation- and gadget-filled environment.

You may pave the path for a better, more balanced relationship with technology by putting these useful suggestions into practice. By doing so, you'll make sure that the digital era improves our lives while preserving our well-being.

www.ingramcontent.com/pod-product-compliance
Lightning Source LLC
LaVergne TN
LVHW041221050326
832903LV00021B/729